STRANGE LYRE

THE PENTECOSTALIZATION
OF EVANGELICAL WORSHIP

DAVID DE BRUYN

AFTERWORD BY SCOTT ANIOL

 Press

Published by G3 Press
4979 GA-5
Douglasville, GA 30135
www.G3Min.org

Printed in the United States of America by Graphic Response, Atlanta, GA.

ISBN: 978-1-959908-19-7

Cover Design: Scott Schaller

Contents

Contents

Introduction

It's hardly disputable that global Christianity has been overwhelmed and colonized by the Pentecostal and charismatic movements. After Roman Catholicism, the Christianity identified variously as charismatic, Pentecostal, Prosperity Gospel, or Latter Rain (with all its permutations and differences) makes up by far the largest percentage of what is classified as Christian. In just over 100 years since its beginnings in Azusa Street, California, it has come to dominate Christianity, and particularly the Christianity spreading in the Global South and Southeast. The growing and new-born Christianity in South America, Africa, and southeast Asia is overwhelmingly of the Pentecostal kind.

Non-Pentecostals, or *cessationists* as they are sometimes called, have dwindled into the minority. Very few voices have been raised to counter the theological distinctives of Pentecostalism: an emphasis on the supernatural sign gifts of the Holy Spirit, a belief in the baptism of the Spirit subsequent to salvation, and assorted novel views on healing, prosperity, and spiritual warfare. A notable exception was John MacArthur's 2013 *Strange Fire* conference and subsequent book, and more recently the 2023 "Cessationist" Film, Tom Pennington's *A Biblical Case for Cessationism*, and the 2024 G3 Ministries Cessationism Conference. But by and large, cessationists simply accept their minority status, and defend their theology when asked.

But perhaps far more insidious has been the quiet takeover of Christian worship by Pentecostalism, even in those churches that reject the theology of continuationism. Worship forms are far more portable than doctrinal statements, and they tend to insinuate themselves gradually and quietly. A popular song, emerging from

Introduction

Pentecostal or charismatic roots, finds a home in cessationist circles, because its theology is either orthodox and acceptable to cessationists, or sufficiently banal to fit in almost anywhere. This is not intrinsically problematic; it simply illustrates how worship forms travel across denominational lines in ways that sermons and Bible studies do not. Of course, some of the most distinctive Pentecostal acts of worship remain out-of-bounds for cessationist churches: praying in tongues, announcing prophecies, public laying on of hands for healings or exorcisms. What arrives incognito is the Pentecostal understanding of the act of corporate worship, with its accompanying postures, approaches, and expectations.

As cessationist churches post vigilant patrols at the doctrinal boundaries, but offer open borders to charismatic songs, music, forms of prayer, and overall sentiment, a quiet transformation takes place. The result is a church that is cessationist on paper, but increasingly charismatic in sentiment and outlook. It is not long before this begins quietly reordering the discipline and ultimately, the doctrine of the church from within. Charles Hodge predicted as much:

> Whenever a change occurs in the religious opinions of a community, it is always preceded by a change in their religious feelings. The natural expression of the feelings of true piety is the doctrines of the Bible. As long as these feelings are retained, these doctrines will be retained; but should they be lost, the doctrines are either held for form's sake or rejected, according to circumstance; and if the feelings again be called into life, the doctrines return as a matter of course.[1]

---

[1] Charles Hodge, "Address to the Students of the Theological Seminary," *Biblical Repertory and Princeton Review* 5 (1829): 92.

Introduction

But what can the "Pentecostalization of worship" refer to, if we have removed the overtly charismatic acts of praying in tongues, healing, and so forth? In this book, I will argue that Pentecostal worship has a matrix of distinctives that is a clear break from historic, Protestant worship, or even the worship that preceded it. These distinctives are not unique to Pentecostalism, and some of them originated before it existed. Nevertheless, they represent much of the spirit of self-identified Pentecostals when it comes to worship, and certainly represent an innovation in Christian worship. I suggest these distinctives are the following:

1. A populist approach to tradition, art, and the ecclesial authority. Populism rejected expert opinion in matters of theology, church order, or music, and promoted the intuitive feelings of the common man as the arbiter of decisions in church—not what had been curated by centuries of use, or chosen by men trained in art and

theology or known to challenge and discipline those who submitted to it was to be included in Christian worship, but what was experienced as immediately intelligible and accessible or found to be widely popular by people of all states and tastes. Pentecostalism has been, and remains, overtly populist in outlook, approach, and sentiment.

2. Praise and worship theology. This is a peculiarly charismatic approach to worship that believes in an almost sacramental view of music and a tangible experience of the Holy Spirit's presence. By means of successive phases of music and songs, often repetitive and unbroken in sequence, worshipers can be led deeper and deeper into the presence of God, until worshipers experience the presence of God in felt, experiential ways. Certain kinds of music or prayer will bring about God's presence, the way the Mass brought the body and blood of Christ to the Table.

3. An emphasis on extemporaneity and intensity. Pentecostalism's emphasis on the Holy Spirit often includes the belief that spontaneity and extemporaneity represent yieldedness to the Spirit, whereas what is prepared, scripted, or planned represents "the dead letter" or "quenching the Spirit." Working hand-in-hand with extemporaneity is *intensity*, the belief that real spiritual experience is found in the closed-eye, swaying search for intense intimacy with God, often felt in deeply personal, and even private ways. This intensity is what aestheticians and philosophers refer to as Dionysian—as opposed to Apollonian—sentiment.

As we will see, each of these three represent a break from historic Christian worship, which emphasized both beauty and simplicity, maintained a gospel-shaped worship service, and sought a carefully planned, corporate, and Apollonian expression of worship.

Early Beginnings
of Pentecostal Worship

An easy error for a historian to commit is to equate or link events or movements in history that are similar, while ignoring or underplaying their differences. One example of this is when historians of worship note that modern negative reactions to contemporary pop-rock worship contain similar objections to ones levelled against the hymns of Martin Luther, and later, Charles Wesley and Isaac Watts. Without question, there are similarities. What a lazy historian fails to notice is when the differences are greater than the similarities.

That can be said about the roots of Pentecostal worship, found in the populist religious mood that swept America in the late 1780s through to the nineteenth century. Yes, there are many parallels to earlier reactions against ossified liturgical forms that sparked more colloquial and lay-driven worship (e.g. some Waldensians and Lollards, some Anabaptists, the Moravians). But there are differences to previous reformations of worship that far outweigh the similarities. When we examine those differences, we will find that the seedbed from which Pentecostalism grew in the 1900s was actually a considerable departure from prior worship reformers such as Luther, Wesley, and Watts.

Nathan Hatch detects four waves of populist folk religious music in America from 1780 to 1830.[1] The first was among Separatist Baptists in rural New England. Some of the early hymnals of these Baptists maintained continuity with the hymns of Watts and others, but a flood of hymnbooks published by Elias Smith between 1804 and 1820 contained no overlap with the

---

[1] Nathan O. Hatch, *The Democratization of American Christianity* (New Haven, CT: Yale University Press, 1991).

accepted hymnals of the day. Original and catchy lyrics linked to popular folk tunes became the new tradition of rural New England Baptists.

The second wave of populist worship was Methodist revivalism. The Wesleys had taught the importance of the participation of all people, but had also insisted that hymns maintain dignity and reverence. But Methodism in America during the early 1800s went in a new direction. It included spontaneous song, shouting, jumping, and seeking a rousing emotional response to the singing. These songs were the beginnings of the "gospel song": simple, easily remembered lyrics, verses written in rhyming pairs with a chorus or refrain. Gospel songs were songs of testimony, marching songs of solidarity, humorous ballads, even appeals to repentance. These gospel songs became the basis of best-selling hymnals, and such was the popularity of these gospel songs that publishers of more established hymnals felt constrained to include some of them, with an accompanying apology in the introduction for carrying sub-standard hymnody.

The third wave was the black spiritual. Baptist and Methodist evangelism among slaves encouraged congregational composing of songs and the use of tunes familiar to them. The songs were, in the words of an observer, "short scraps of disjointed affirmations, pledges, or prayers, lengthened out with long repetitious choruses ... sung in the merry chorus-manner of the southern harvest field, or husking-frolic method." The music was unusually percussive, syncopated, using complex rhythms and polymeter, with overlapping call and response patterns.

The Mormons constituted the fourth wave of popular religious song. Greatly familiar with popular culture, the Mormons transformed ballads, folk music, and patriotic songs into Mormon hymns that promoted specifically Mormon doctrine.

Before the American Civil War broke out, this outpouring of populist worship had co-opted and entered popular culture. This music and poetry were not fashioned by trained musicians and poets for the improvement of others. It reveled in its rugged, raw, and unshapely origin and form: it was "earthen vessels carrying the glory of the Lord," the "salt of the earth speaking truth in childlike fashion." American Christianity was permanently marked by this populism, and since Protestantism all but died in Europe in the nineteenth and twentieth centuries, the Christianity that was exported to the rest of the world retained this flavor.

Pentecostalism grew out of the Holiness movement, and thus drank deeply from the populist movements in Methodism, Baptist, and African American circles. Charles Fox Parham (1873-

1929), is usually credited with the beginnings of the movement. He was born in Muscatine, IA, and claimed a revelation of light at age 13. Parham associated with Methodism but rejected their hierarchy and moved toward holiness theology. He broke with Methodism in 1895 and established his own ministry, Bethel Bible College, in October 1900. He emphasized "primitive Christianity." In December 1900, he gave his students the homework assignment of studying the baptism of the Holy Spirit, while he was away in Kansas City. At New Year's Eve service 1901, Agnes Ozman supposedly spoke in tongues, in Chinese.

The school closed so Parham and his students could travel. The school reopened in Houston, Texas, and influenced William J. Seymour (1870–1922), who took the movement to Los Angeles. Seymour was the son of freed slaves. He was raised a Baptist but claimed dreams and visions as a youth. Seymour met Parham and embraced his views. Parham was actually something of a racist and would not worship with blacks.

Seymour started Azusa Street Mission at 312 Azusa Street, Los Angeles, which purportedly experienced a revival (1906-1909). From 1906 to 1914, Azusa Street became known for its ecstatic utterances, dramatic worship, and unorthodox behaviors. It attracted observers and participants from around the world. By 1907, the movement had over 13,000 adherents.

The great irony is that the "new" movement was only relatively new. It was a blend of Baptist, Methodist, and Negro-spiritual populist worship that had spread across the American frontier for the previous century. Ecstatic utterances, spontaneous exclamations, and popular music combined with catchy lyrics was not a new work of the Spirit. It was a fairly established work of American populism and pragmatism that was about to become a worldwide phenomenon.

Pentecostal "Praise and Worship": A Radical Departure from Historic Worship

Christian worship has often had a remarkably similar shape across traditions. Bryan Chapell showed in his work *Christ-Centered Worship* that corporate worship (sans communion) in Roman, Lutheran, Reformed, and Evangelical traditions had a very similar form: a Call to Worship, a Kyrie or Confession, followed by Thanksgiving, an Old Testament reading, a New Testament reading, a prayer for Illumination, a Sermon, followed by a Benediction or dismissal, with hymns or psalms interspersed. Communion services also followed a similar pattern: An Invitation, Preparatory hymn, a Consecration of elements, an Exhortation of preparation, the Words of Institution, Breaking of bread, Communion, a psalm or hymn, thanksgiving prayer, and Benediction.[1]

Friends and proponents of Pentecostal worship often do not realize how radically different charismatic worship is from this historic pattern. Pentecostal authors have written that praise is a kind of "path" into the presence of God. That is, worship is not a series of gracious revelations from God's Word with faith-responses from his people. Worship becomes a series of steps or stages, growing in intimacy and intensity. Charismatic worship writers speak of the importance of "flow": a technique of uninterrupted, continual music, designed to emotionally transport the worshipers into the climactic experience of "worship," which they deem to be more intense and focused than "praise."

---

[1] For a biblical explanation of this historic, gospel-shaped worship, see Scott Aniol, *Biblical Foundations of Corporate Worship* (Conway, AR: Free Grace Press, 2022).

Charismatic theologians do not base this on any Old or New Testament narratives of worship, such as Exodus 19-24 or Isaiah 6. Instead, an entirely new model of worship, known as the "Tabernacle Model" or "Five Phase Model" is used, using fragments of phrases from the Psalms. First, there is Invitation, "songs of personal testimony in the camp." This is followed by Engagement, "through the gates with thanksgiving." Third comes Exaltation, "into his courts with praise." Fourth is Adoration, "solemn worship inside the Holy Place." Finally, there is Intimacy, "in the Holy of Holies." Of course, this is a technique in search of a text, not any serious attempt to mimic biblical forms. Nothing that Israel did in corporate worship even vaguely corresponds to the pursuit of a heightening climactic worship.

Indeed, charismatic theologians have changed the meaning of the worship service. Biblically and historically, a worship service is where God's people *respond* corporately to what God has revealed about himself. Yes, this response ought to be heartfelt, sincere, meaningful, and unfeigned. In charismatic worship theology, one is not so much in pursuit of a *response*, as one is in pursuit of an *experience*: an experience of the presence of God that is intense, sensorily tangible, and emotionally or physically ecstatic. Very importantly, this experience will be almost passively felt, once the moment arrives, as opposed to a rational response to God's Word.

In making this the highpoint of worship, Pentecostal worship is dabbling with two very dangerous, and unbiblical ideas. First, the Pentecostal approach has parallels to the sensual and ecstatic worship of paganism. The idea that worship must be a steady and growing stimulation has all too familiar and uncomfortable parallels with the approaches of everything from the Israelites around the golden calf, to the prophets of Baal, to shamanism and trance-inducing rituals of false religion. The methods among these may be diverse, but the approach is similar: steadily stimulate the body into a heightened state through sensual music, dance, or movement, while steadily sedating the mind through chant-like repetition, narrowed focus, or hallucinogenic drugs, until the goal is reached: climactic encounter or possession with the spirit/god, the whole ritual consciously or unconsciously mimicking sexual stimulation and climax. By contrast, Hebrew and Christian worship has always required the frequent conscious response of the mind and will, the restraining of what could become sensual, modesty in bodily expression, and a rational, active response to God, not a sensual, passive one.

Second, the Pentecostal approach treats music with the same sacramentality that perverted the Lord's Table into the Roman Mass. Sacramentalism is the error of believing that the communion cup and bread turn into the actual body and blood of the Lord by an act of grace apart from faith. The sacraments are "*ex opere operato*"—they work and confer grace independently of the priests or recipients. That kind of sacramentalism is precisely how charismatic theology treats music in the worship service: a belief that apart from the Word rightly divided and rightly received, the music may bring about the felt presence of God for those hearing it. The music "ushers" people into God's manifest presence, and God may manifest himself, the way he did when the little bell was rung at Mass. The music has an independent power, and as one Charismatic theologian put it, "the flow should move naturally (using connections from the songs' content, keys, and tempos); and the flow should move toward a goal of a climatic experience of true worship of God."[2] This is not

---

[2] David Blomgren, *The Song of the Lord* (1978), as described in Swee Hong Lim and Lester Ruth, *Lovin' on Jesus: A*

music as a form of congregational prayer, a conscious corporate response of faith-filled prayer to what God has revealed in his Word.

When Christian worship is Pentecostalized, it is not merely a "style" or "preference" that has changed. The point and goal of Christian worship has been altered; and the very shape of active call-and-response has been substituted with a passive stimulatory-ecstatic model. This is no small change.

Concise History of Contemporary Worship (Nashville: Abingdon Press, 2017), 33.

The Idols of Intensity
and Extemporaneity

A polarized debate goes on between different
stripes of Christians over the place of experience
in Christianity. One side asserts that experiential
faith (what the Puritans used to call "experi-
mental religion") is fundamental to a living, su-
pernaturally-empowered relationship with
Christ. The other side asserts that experiential religion is of passing interest, for spiritual experiences range from the genuinely God-given to the
wildly false and even demonic, and vary widely
among different personality-types. Ultimately,
say these Christians, what matters is allegiance to
truth, both in belief and behavior.

In moments of clarity, we agree with both
sides, because we are aware of what each side is
against: dead formalism ("a straight as a gun bar-
rel theologically, and as empty as one spiritually,"

said one) and untethered spiritual adventures ("glandular religion," as coined by another). Pentecostalism's strongest selling point has been the supposed vividness of its promised supernatural experiences, both in corporate and private worship. The idea of direct revelation, ecstatic utterances, and marvelous deliverances present a kind of Christianity that appears enviably immediate, sensorily overpowering, and almost irrefutably persuasive. Particularly for Christians coming from a religious background of set forms, liturgical routines, and even unregenerate leadership, the contrast appears to be one of old and false versus new and true.

Sadly, many true believers within Pentecostalism find out within a short space that the promise of overwhelming spiritual experiences begins to lack luster after a time, and the corporate worship in pursuit of spontaneous spiritual highs can become as tedious and predictable as a service read verbatim from a prayer book. Pentecostalism's pursuit of intensity and spontaneity in worship turns out to be an idol that both cheats and forsakes its worshipers.

Deeply embedded in the Pentecostal psyche is the idea that the Spirit of God is wedded to spontaneity and freedom of form. It is the very "openness" to his movements, unrestricted by an order of service or set forms of prayer, that supposedly invites his unpredictable arrival, manifested in intense, even ecstatic, spiritual experience. Being spontaneous and extemporaneous demonstrates "openness" and "receptivity," whereas insisting upon our own forms quenches what the Spirit may wish to do.

Similar to this is the notion, almost unquestioned in Pentecostal thinking, that for a spiritual experience to be real, it must be *felt*. That is, *intensity is the mark of authenticity*. When the Spirit manifests himself, the worshiper should expect some kind of moment of feeling deeply loved, close to God, or intimacy. The pursuit of a Pentecostal worship service is the experience of intense intimacy.

Errors are only compelling to the degree that they contain some vital truth, now heavily distorted. The truth is that both extemporaneity and some form of intense spiritual experience are part of true, living Christianity. The problem is when the experience of intensity is sought for its own sake, and when the method of extemporaneity becomes a tool to manipulate the Spirit (whom we supposedly agree cannot be manipulated or controlled; John 3:8).

Intensity of spiritual experience ebbs and flows, like all emotional intensity. The man who is forever in pursuit of his fading feelings of dizzy infatuation with a woman is an infant in an adult body, trying to hang onto what is meant to lead him on to loves that are both stronger and more serene. In wanting to pickle an experience so that we may open and enjoy it at any time, we distort and destroy the very experience. We make an idol of a pleasure, and its revenge upon us is to become less pleasing each time. Trying to capture intense spiritual experience in every corporate worship service is as tiresome as a man trying to reproduce the precise circumstances of his first date with his now-wife, and doing so every Friday night, in hopes of "re-capturing the spark." Sentimental-ism is more than feeling; it is trying to "feel our feelings" and lather in the pleasure of a feeling. But unavoidably, and ironically, when we pursue intensity in worship, we have shifted the focus from God himself to a supposed experience of God.

Similarly, some kind of extemporaneity rep-resents engagement with and understanding of what we are doing and saying in worship. Rare is the preacher who prays and preaches without the slightest deviation from his scripted prayers and fine-tuned manuscript. Such a man soon begins to sound like a spiritual jukebox, and his congregation tunes him out. However structured our services, we must be *in* them, and mean them, and speak in our own voices. Extemporaneity, like intensity, is a good thing in moderation.

The Pentecostal error is to confuse preparedness with independence, thinking that extemporaneity represents trust in God, a willingness to say and speak only as directed in the moment, while preparedness is rooted in pride and self-reliance. In this way of thinking, preparedness is actually an affront to God, or an act of pride, or an unwillingness to be childlike and pliable during corporate worship. Of course, no Pentecostal congregation are absolute purists in this regard. That is, a consistent application of the principle would mean singing songs without pre-set lyrics with music composed in the moment, sermons made up on the spot, and so on.

Again, we can acknowledge the truth: some preparedness can be a refusal to pray and trust God. But the correction of that error is to prepare *and* pray, not to eschew preparation altogether. Indeed, the Spirit of God rides best in his own chariot, the Word he inspired. Therefore, the more the Word of God dwells richly (Col. 3:16) in our hymns, prayers, and sermons, the more filled with the Spirit we will be (Eph 5:18-19).

Nothing But Feelings

Pentecostal worship places great emphasis on intensity. By *intensity*, they mean a strongly felt experience of emotion, intimacy, joy, wonder, or happiness. Indeed, this is a close cousin of the *ecstasy* in ecstatic utterances. The experience sought is one where active seeking gives way to a passive experience of overwhelming pleasure or emotion.

Critically examining emotional experiences like this has all the fun of ruining someone's birthday surprise or spoiling a joke by blabbing the punchline before the narrator has finished. We don't like people like that, who appear to find joy in lessening the joy of others. Not surprisingly, when a critique of someone's spiritual experiences begins, the response is often an impatient sentiment along the lines of "Can't you just let people have their fun?" or, "What's it to you if someone has a different worship experience to you?"

But in matters of Christian worship, we cannot be content if worshipers merely make the claim to an ecstatic experience. That's precisely because the *experience of worship is not the goal of worship*. Worship is not successful simply because the worshipers enjoyed their worship. Christian worship is rooted in truth, and therefore everything that claims to be Christian worship must be a truthful response to a truthful revelation of the true God. In other words, you can get worship wrong, even if it felt right. Many people feel good about an exam they wrote and find out they failed; some feel terrible and find out they passed with flying colors. The indispensable necessity of Christian worship is a true revelation of God from the Scriptures, and a truthful—that is, appropriate and corresponding—response to that revelation. The First Commandment restricts worship to the true God. The Second Commandment restricts the responses of worship to those he has commanded, which correspond to his being. The true God worshiped the true way constitutes biblical worship.

This brings us to a rather dispassionate discussion of felt emotions in worship, one that is sure to annoy all fans of scrunchy-face worship. Philosophers and thinkers have written much on how human emotions differ: their categories, their manifestations, and how they are evoked. Dating back to classical Greece, philosophers have often placed emotions into two categories: those evoked by reason, and those evoked by physical sensation. Different nomenclature has been used, but a similar idea prevailed for centuries. Premodern theologians spoke of the *affections* and the *passions*. Nietzsche coined the terms *Apollonian* and *Dionysian*. Our own era has collapsed the two into the word *emotion*, but the distinction is worth reviving and keeping.

After all, the Bible makes the same distinction. It speaks of those who are controlled by their bodily feelings (Phil 3:19; Rom 8:5, 16:18). They are *psyuchikoi*, the soulish ones, controlled and dominated by appetite. By contrast, it speaks of those controlled by a renewed mind, and by the Spirit in our spirits (Rom 8:5, Gal 5:16; 1 Cor 2:15). The *pneumatikoi*, the spiritual ones, are not manipulated by bodily feelings, but by affections and minds set above (Col 3:2). Let no one misunderstand. This is not the Gnostic dualism that pitted the body against the spirit. This is a biblical distinction between those who are controlled by rational submission to God in his Word and those who are controlled (more accurately, manipulated) by the whims of a worldly desire for the temporal pleasures of food, sex, excitement, or euphoria.

What does this have to do with the intensity that Pentecostal worship seeks? Consider: is the intensity of Pentecostal worship a rational response of the heart, or is it a sensation? Is it evoked by consideration of truth, or charmed by a combination of chord progressions? Is the goal to rightly value and admire God, or to feel my feelings?

The fact that the intensity that is sought is felt so acutely in the body (hence the intensity), the fact that is often evoked without much understanding or meditation on revealed truth, the fact that the participant often feels passive and overwhelmed, would lead many observers, ancient and modern, to classify Pentecostal intensity as a passion, as Dionysian, or even as sensual. Furthermore, the addiction that many have to it has all the signs of people who have found an emotional stimulant.

By contrast, Christian worship has to first pass through the filter of a Spirit-filled understanding. It must respond submissively, which means humbly, soberly, and reverently. That also means such a response is modest, because humility, almost by definition, is not flamboyant or outrageous. Worship like this is "Apollonian": it creates some distance between mind and body, because the mind is reflecting on truth, not being manipulated by what the body (the ear) is finding sensuous pleasure in. Certainly, the response may be robust, triumphant, and filled to the brim with zeal. But it is always a response that the spirit is making to the Holy Spirit's illumination. It is never an irrational feeling of pleasure that sweeps upon one because of a combination of chords, rhythms, nostalgia, lighting, breathy and crooning vocals, or some other sensual trick. Those are marionette strings, attempting to pull on the appetites directly.

The worship of the true God is persuasive, not manipulative. God persuades us to admire, by revealing his beauty in his Word. False gods manipulate by placing audio-visual candy canes in front of our noses and ears. Persuasive worship is by nature, then, "slower," requiring more time, concentration, and focus, for no one can be persuaded without some rational thought. Those addicted to manipulative worship instinctively call persuasive worship "boring." Indeed, would a toddler prefer a forty-minute explanation of the wonders of galactic supernovae over a cartoon? Manipulative worship impatiently skips the slow and deep persuasion of the human spirit (knowing full well that it will not be popular with the masses). It will give us the intensity our bodies crave, regardless of the object of our worship. When it comes to what Pentecostals call "intensity," we would do well to distinguish persuasive, spirit-centered zeal from a manipulative, sensually-controlled passion.

Cessmaticism: The Strange Hybrid of Contemporary Christian Worship

We began by making the claim that Pentecostalism has quietly (or not so quietly) colonized Protestant worship, even in those churches and groups that explicitly reject Pentecostal theology. We have described the distinctives of Pentecostal worship, not in terms of its views regarding the operation of the charismatic gifts, but in terms of its focus on intensity, spontaneity, and its distinctive "praise-and-worship" theology of worship. It now remains to make the case that these approaches are widely shared and practiced in non-charismatic, or cessationist circles.

In the first place, there is little doubt that what is prized as "intensity" in Pentecostal circles is fairly well accepted as a laudable goal in cessationist evangelical circles. The move towards intensity is seen in many a non-charismatic church's method of singing one song after another, in rapid succession, only the occasional musician's deejay vocals over the bridge intro. The practice of singing five, six, or more songs one after the other, apart from causing some of the elderly to just eventually sit down during the songs out of sheer pain and frustration, is closer to the "flow-like" worship of Praise and Worship theology than like a thoughtful response to God's Word. The choice of songs also appears suspiciously like the Praise and Worship, Five-Stage theology of the charismatics. Beginning with upbeat, thanksgiving songs, reaching a crescendo of triumphalism, and then gliding down into the zone of breathy, "deep" songs of intimacy just before the offering or sermon.

A second mark of the takeover of worship by charismatics is that non-charismatic evangelicals are drawn to rather uncritically embrace the music of charismatic songwriters. Of course, several of the modern hymns written by those in openly charismatic circles (such as Sovereign Grace) or "cautious-but-open" circles qualify as decent or even good hymns, having both theologically sturdy lyrics and readily likeable and singable melodies. There is little wonder that many of our churches sing them, for their lyrics are often without cliches, and their music answers to twenty-first-century musical sensibilities.

The problem is not the contemporary nature of these songs. It does not matter if a song was written in 221, 1021, or 2021, as long as it is true, good, and beautiful. The problem is not even the charismatic commitments or associations of the songwriters. Enough beautiful hymns were written by people whose theology we do not all share, for example Charles Wesley, Nikolaus von Zinzendorf, Paul Gerhardt, or Frederick Faber.

The problem is far more that on the spectrum of Apollonian to Dionysian sentiment, they probably lean closer to the Dionysian side, at least musically. This is not surprising, given what we have seen regarding Pentecostal approaches to emotion and intensity. In a non-charismatic church, skillful musicians can interpret some of these songs and hymns in a fashion that communicates sobriety and modesty, and so may make these works practical and helpful for a church seeking reverent worship. This is something that Luther did with the secular tunes that he employed as hymns. Thoughtful pastors can thus use these alongside a healthy diet of excellent, classical hymns that balance out the passionate, Dionysian element, both musically, and lyrically. My own church has attempted to attain this balance.

In practice, this is not often what happens. Instead, I've witnessed first-hand at least three results. First, there is a push to perform these songs with the kind of t-shirt-and-jeans folksiness that seems to accompany the more passionate nature of the music. That produces the very opposite of disciplining these hymns into a more sober form; it ends up re-shaping the whole music team into a less formal, more band-like atmosphere. For good reason: some hymns simply don't suit the "worship-band," and some hymns simply don't suit an organ or a grand piano and strings. If some hymns seem like they belong in a tux, and others seem like they belong in beach shorts and sandals, there's probably something to that. We'd do well to ask exactly why that is, and not dismiss the question while sprinting off to buy a Fender Stratocaster for the dudes up front.

Second, the more these Dionysian-dominant songs are sung, the more they tend to choke out older and classical hymnody. Unless the pastors have a strong sense of what music communicates, they will be led by the same appetitive pull that passion-centered music has on all. They will see how much the congregants enjoy such songs; they will interpret this enjoyment as "connecting meaningfully" with the music, and notice how the visceral response is absent in some of the more Apollonian classic hymns. They will take the lyrical content as the entire meaning of the hymn, and the music as the amoral preference of the congregation, and eventually allow that preference to dominate. Consequently, classic hymns will steadily die out. If left to a popular vote, popular entertainment will win against serious formation one hundred percent of the time, and Christian songs shaped into the saccharine forms of pop-rock will trounce older, sober tunes every time.

Third, because of this choke effect of charismatic-type songs on older hymnody, the congregation finds itself increasingly cut off from the tradition of Christian worship. They do not know it, but they are drifting further from the worship *lingua franca* of their forebearers, and becoming cut off from the images, metaphors, and language of centuries of Christian worship. That alienation goes deeper than memory of hymn lyrics. It is a growing alienation from the very rhythms and shape of historic Christian worship, a growing distance from the affections that Christians have shared for centuries. Without the Christian tradition, there is nothing to balance the congregation from the excesses and blind spots of contemporary Christianity, so the worship errors of our day (narcissism, sentimentalism) are only compounded and reinforced each week. Within a few years, the congregation is now a strange animal. From the pulpit, they may still be perpetuating an ancient, confessional doctrinal tradition. But from a liturgical and worship point of view, they are radical innovators—they cannot trace their worship practices further back than a few decades. They may believe very similar things to their confessional forebears, but there is little doubt that they feel very differently than their ancestors did about those same truths. Their affections have been catechized with the passionate music of pop-rock, which has shaped their very posture towards the truth they profess. They may be non-charismatics with their lips, but their hearts are with Pentecostal worship. The mind may be cessationist, but the imagination is charismatic.

Conclusion

A good theologian once drew me a diagram of the progress of Christian doctrine and Christian history from the apostles to our day. He drew a rather jagged line, with offshoots and branches coming off it. He explained, "The line from the apostles to us today is not a straight one. It includes many errors, corrections, over-corrections, and responses to those over-corrections. The line of orthodoxy therefore is never a perfectly straight line of ascent—it is as jagged as all the movements away from and back towards orthodoxy. Along the way, there are genuine departures from the faith—actual heresies that veer off far from the faith—those are the far-flung branches breaking off from the jagged line. It's important to distinguish when something is a true departure from the faith, or when it is a reaction within orthodoxy needing its own correction."

The same line could be drawn for worship. Christian worship over the centuries has been the same jagged line of errors, corrections, reactions, overreactions, and so forth. These have included controversies such as the use of musical instruments, the singing of psalms only or hymns and psalms, the question of ministerial robes, the presence of images in the meeting place, and several other disputes. Sometimes there have been genuine worship heresies: the worship of Mary as an intercessor, or the Mass as the body and blood of Christ available for the expiation of sins.

Where does Pentecostalism fall on these jagged lines? On the theological side, Pentecostalism's errors are serious, though not fatal. That is, erroneous teaching on the Holy Spirit and the charismatic gifts represent significant deviations in the whole body of orthodox Christian doctrine, but they do not constitute a denial of the gospel (that is, unless a proponent articulates them so, as in the man who says you must speak in tongues to be saved, or experience a baptism of the Spirit to be truly regenerate). As long as Pentecostals profess the gospel of salvation by grace alone through faith alone in Christ alone, they remain brothers and sisters in Christ.

However, errors are seldom stable things. They have trajectories, and the general trajectories of Pentecostal errors in the last century have been bad fruit: the Prosperity Gospel, the Toronto Blessing, and all the extremes that have accompanied those. A good tree brings forth good fruit, and so on.

Pentecostal worship is not quite as simple, for it has been unruly and unbiblical right out of the gate. Birthed in the heady revivalism of the American frontier, it has remained committed to novelty, spontaneity, and extemporaneity as marks of "fresh wind" or the true leading of the Holy Spirit. While leaders of "conservative Pentecostalism" speak out against the excesses in charismaticism, one can't help feeling that this is like the owner of a tavern complaining that his patrons are making a racket once outside his respectable establishment. What the parents do in moderation, the children do in excess. If Pentecostal worship was decent and in order from the get-go, its proponents should have no problem with how it is developed by the next generation. But instead, the tree has borne fruit in keeping with its nature. Worship that was never regulated by the clear prescriptions of God's Word has license to innovate, and to innovate as wildly as the ecstatic worship demands. What began in 1900 as errors in understanding the apostolic sign gifts have become full-blown heterodox worship: people barking like dogs, uncontrolled laughter and weeping, or other acts that look far more like demons making sport of people than of Christian worship.

Conclusion

But it is not these heresies that flame out and explode in a few years that deserve our guarded attention. Their very wackiness makes them easily detectable to most. The greater concern is those non-charismatic churches that have adjusted the rudder of their ship ever so slightly in the direction of the charismatic flavor of worship. A 2-degree course change is barely noticeable in the short term. But it begins to become felt after a few years, noticeable after ten, clear after fifteen, and permanent after twenty. The longer the distance you travel, the greater that minor course correction begins to affect your location relative to orthodoxy and orthopathy.

What begins as slightly modified liturgy becomes an altered feel of corporate worship. Often enough, this begins to change the approach to ministry itself. Explosive numerical growth pushes leaders to consider dropping those denominational labels that alienate, and rename (read: rebrand) the church. Before long, the church's more detailed confession of faith is abridged to help seekers feel less threatened. Finally, doctrines that were formerly preached against or denied by the church's original statement of faith now have a home in the church's now "broader orthodoxy." In this scenario, it is not a change in doctrine that changes the worship. It is a subtle drift in worship that eventually changes the doctrine.

It would be consoling to say that such a scenario is a strange anomaly and that such things hardly ever happen to orthodox, biblical churches. But most of us, without even racking our brains, can name several churches that travelled precisely along the path I've described. Once again, the prescient words of Charles Hodge in 1829: "Whenever a change occurs in the religious *opinions* of a community, it is always preceded by a change in their religious *feelings*. The natural expression of the feelings of true piety is the doctrines of the Bible. *As long as these feelings are retained, these doctrines will be retained;* but should they be lost, the doctrines are either held for form's sake or rejected, according to circumstance; and if the feelings again be called into life, the doctrines return as a matter of course."

Evangelical worship has, for the most part, embraced the "religious feelings" of Pentecostalism. Not surprisingly, charismatic doctrine has begun to capture the theological minds of those who were formerly cessationists. It remains to be seen how much longer those churches that claim to be non-charismatic in doctrine will remain that way, if they persist in embracing the passions and sentiments of Pentecostal worship.

Afterword

The Biblical Alternative: Covenant-Renewal Worship

Scott Aniol

David has done a masterful job in this short work exposing the Pentecostalization of evangelical worship. I wholeheartedly agree with his assessment: most evangelical churches today worship like charismatics whether they affirm explicitly charismatic theology or not.

So what is the alternative? Throughout biblical history and in the early church, churches practiced what is sometimes called "covenant-renewal worship." Worship in the Middle Ages broke from this theology and devolved into a sacramentalism rooted in mystical experience not unlike the experience-driven worship of contemporary evangelicalism. But one of the most significant

Reformation recoveries of the sixteenth and seventeenth centuries was a return to biblical covenant-renewal worship.

This biblical theology of worship considers the Lord's Day corporate gathering to be one of covenant renewal in which God renews his covenant with his people through the gospel, and his people renew their covenant with him in responses of adoration, confession, thanksgiving, and dedication. This kind of covenant renewal glorifies God because it highlights the work that he has done, and it sanctifies his people to mature in how they live out the implications of that gospel covenant—corporate worship disciples believers to live as worshipers unto his glory. Here's how I describe it in *Biblical Foundations of Corporate Worship*:

> Corporate worship is like renewing our gospel vows to Christ. Just like when we were first converted, God calls us to draw near to him.

Just like at our conversion, we respond with confession of sin and acknowledgement that we have broken God's laws. Just like when we were first saved, we hear words of pardon from God because of the sacrifice of Christ. Just like when we began our relationship with God, we eagerly listen to his instructions and commit to obey. We are not getting "re-saved" each week, but we are renewing our covenant vows to the Lord, and in so doing, we are re-kindling our relationship with him and our commitment to him, and he with us.

Worship services shaped by this theology follow the shape of the gospel:

God reveals himself and calls his people to worship through his Word.

God's people acknowledge and confess their need for forgiveness.

God provides atonement.

God speaks his Word.

God's people respond with commitment.

God hosts a celebratory feast.

Corporate worship that embodies this theology is dialogical, a conversation between God and his people. God always speaks first through his Word, and then his people respond appropriately to God's revelation.

This theology of worship is rooted in the conviction that the biblical purpose of corporate worship is not primarily authentic experience; rather, the purpose of corporate worship is the disciplined formation of God's people into those who will live lives of worship. As Paul stresses in 1 Corinthians 14, the only complete chapter in the

New Testament dedicated to the subject of corporate worship, all things "when you come together" must be done for building up (vv. 3, 4, 5, 6, 9, 12, 17, 19, 26). A worship service is first and foremost a meeting that God has called with his people so that he might speak his Words to us for the upbuilding and edification of his people.

In a corporate worship service, we are not the primary actors; corporate worship is not primarily us performing for God—that is paganism. A theology of worship that says corporate worship is primarily about us performing for God is still man-centered—it's about what we are doing. A properly God-centered theology of worship will recognize that in a corporate worship service, God is the primary actor. As Christ says to the Samaritan woman in John 4, God is the seeker. God is the initiator. It is God who calls us to draw near to him; we do not invite him to come down to us. It is God who speaks to us first; only then do we respond back to him.

Yes, God deserves our worship, but that's true of all of life. The purpose of a corporate worship service is for God to form the kind of worshipers he deserves. Our responses toward God are essential to true worship, but that is not where worship begins. Worship begins with God speaking through his Word. And furthermore, we need to recognize that our natural, "authentic" responses of worship need to be sanctified. Our understanding of God and our affections toward him must be sanctified as God's Word teaches us, reproves us, corrects us, and trains us in righteousness. Only as we are edified by God's Word are we able to worship him acceptably.

And so one of the fundamental purposes of a corporate worship service is for that kind of sanctification to take place. The primary emphasis in a church gathering ought to be God's Word forming us into acceptable worshipers. This is the commission given to churches by Christ, after all: make disciples.

This is the essence of covenant-renewal worship: disciplined formation. We come to worship to be built up by God's Word, to be formed into the image of Christ by God's Word, to have our affections sanctified anew by the God's Word. We come to a corporate worship service so that our responses of worship—our lives of worship—might be shaped by God's Word. And so our primary concern in a corporate worship service should not simply be authentic expression of worship toward God but rather how the service is edifying us, how it is cultivating our relationship with God and forming us to be the kind of mature disciple-worshipers Scripture commands.

It is not biblical to place priority in corporate worship upon the individual authentic expression of worshipers. No, in biblical worship the emphasis is placed upon the corporate edification of the congregation as God speaks to us through his Word read, preached, prayed, and sung—everything about a biblical worship service ought to mold and shape us into the kinds of people who will worship God acceptably each and every day of the week.

As I trace in *Changed from Glory into Glory: The Liturgical Story of the Christian Faith*, covenant-renewal worship characterized believers in the early church and Protestants following the sixteenth- and seventeenth-century Reformation. Though differences certainly exist between various groups stemming from the Reformation, their theology of covenant-renewal worship was fairly consistent. Another book that very helpfully explains this historic theology of worship is Jonathan Cruse's *What Happens When We Worship*.

Songs within this covenant-renewal worship serve one of two functions: (1) Often psalms and hymns serve as God's words to us, either directly quoting from or paraphrasing Scripture itself. (2) Psalms and hymns can also serve as our response to God's revelation. With both cases, choice of songs depends upon how the lyrical content fits within the dialogical, gospel-shaped covenant renewal service. Songs are not lumped together into a musical "set" in order to create a mood or stimulate emotion; rather, songs are interspersed with Scripture readings and prayers throughout the dialogical, gospel-shaped service.

The music itself is actually not very prominent in this theology of worship. Music is important—it provides an interpretation of the theology of the lyrics and gives expression to that interpretation. But music is secondary. The music is selected and performed to modestly support the truth with sentiments that "accord with sound doctrine" (Tit 2:1), and an emphasis is given to reverence, self-control, sobriety, and dignity in how the songs are led, accompanied, and performed.

Contrary to caricatures, this kind of covenant renewal worship is deeply emotional, but the music is not intended to *immediately stimulate* or *arouse* emotion; rather, deep affections of the soul are stirred by the Holy Spirit through his Word, and music simply gives language to appropriate responses to the Word. Emotion in covenant-renewal worship is not often immediate, visceral, or flashy—rather, it is felt deeply in the soul.

In fact, particularly because of commands in Scripture (like in Titus 2) that Christians are to be dignified and self-controlled, care is given in covenant renewal worship to avoid music that would cause a worshiper to lose control. Christians with this theology recognized that although physical feelings are good, they must be controlled lest our "belly" (a Greek metaphor for bodily passions) be our god (Phil 3:19). Rather, since reverence, dignity, and self-control are qualities that accord with sound doctrine, music is chosen that will nurture and cultivate these qualities and the affections of the soul like compassion, kindness, humility, meekness, and patience (Col 3:12) and love, joy, peace, patience, kindness, goodness, faithfulness, gentleness, and self-control (Gal 5:23). This theology takes note of the fact that qualities like intensity, passion, enthusiasm, exhilaration, or euphoria are never described in Scripture as qualities to pursue or stimulate, and they are never used to define the nature of spiritual maturity or the essence of worship.

Musical choices from this perspective are not about new vs. old or the canonization of one kind of music; rather, it is about choosing musical forms that best accord with a covenant-renewal theology of worship.

This brings us to the heart of the issue. Here we have two dominant theologies of worship today: one that characterizes corporate worship as a time in which believers meet with God at his invitation so that he might speak to us through his Word, sanctifying our minds and hearts, and so that we might respond with appropriate affections toward him that are being sanctified. On the other hand, we have a theology that characterizes corporate worship as a time in which we come to have an authentic emotional experience, which is largely accomplished through musical stimulation.

We may say that we are not charismatic because we believe miraculous gifts have ceased, but if our worship is filled with charismatic music, what are we forming in our people? As Swee Hong Lim and Lester Ruth demonstrate in *Lovin' on Jesus: A Concise History of Contemporary Worship*, contemporary worship music is an embodiment of a charismatic theology of worship meant to create an emotional experience they believe is the manifest presence of God.

Here, then, is the crisis: that very theology and practice of worship that prizes immediacy, "authenticity," and physical experience inherently works against our biblical mandate to build up the body of Christ to mature manhood. Childishness is characterized by demand for immediate gratification; childishness is characterized by being easily swept up and tossed to and fro; an inward focus on my authentic emotional experience is inherently immature. Immature music and worship fosters immature Christianity.

But mature Christian manhood, which 1 Corinthians 14 so clearly defines as the goal of our church gatherings, will be cultivated when every aspect of our corporate worship fits with that purpose, when it embodies the very qualities of spiritual maturity we are seeking to form.

21811629R00046